82nd AIRBORNE
NORMANDY 1944

Steven Smith

Casemate
PHILADELPHIA & OXFORD

Published in the United States of America and Great
Britain in 2017
by CASEMATE PUBLISHERS
1950 Lawrence Road, Havertown, PA 19083
and 10 Hythe Bridge Street, Oxford, OX1 2EW

ISBN-13: 978-1-61200-536-2
Produced by Greene Media Ltd.

Cataloging-in-publication data is available from the Library
of Congress and the British Library.

10 9 8 7 6 5 4 3 2 1

Printed and bound in China
For a complete list of Casemate titles please contact:
CASEMATE PUBLISHERS (US)
Telephone (610) 853-9131, Fax (610) 853-9146
E-mail: casemate@casematepublishers.com

CASEMATE PUBLISHERS (UK)
Telephone (01865) 241249, Fax (01865) 794449
E-mail: casemate-uk@casematepublishers.co.uk

Acknowledgments
Most of the photos are US Signal Corps images that have
come from a number of sources. Grateful thanks go to
BattlefieldHistorian.com, NARA College Park, MD, and
the George Forty Library.

I'd like to thank, in particular, Les Cruise (82nd Airborne)
and Quorn Village On-line Museum for permission to use
the wartime photo of The Curzon Arms; Adam Berry;
Georgina Maltby at Quorn, Liz at Scraptoft, and the helpful
keyholders at the lovely St. Denys Church in Evington who
opened the church for me and showed me round. As
usual, thanks to Mark Franklin (maps), Ian Hughes
(design concept), Richard Wood and the military
cyclists (particularly Peter Anderson) for photos and
enthusiasm. Much of the information for the maps came
from *Cross-Channel Attack*, see Bibliography.

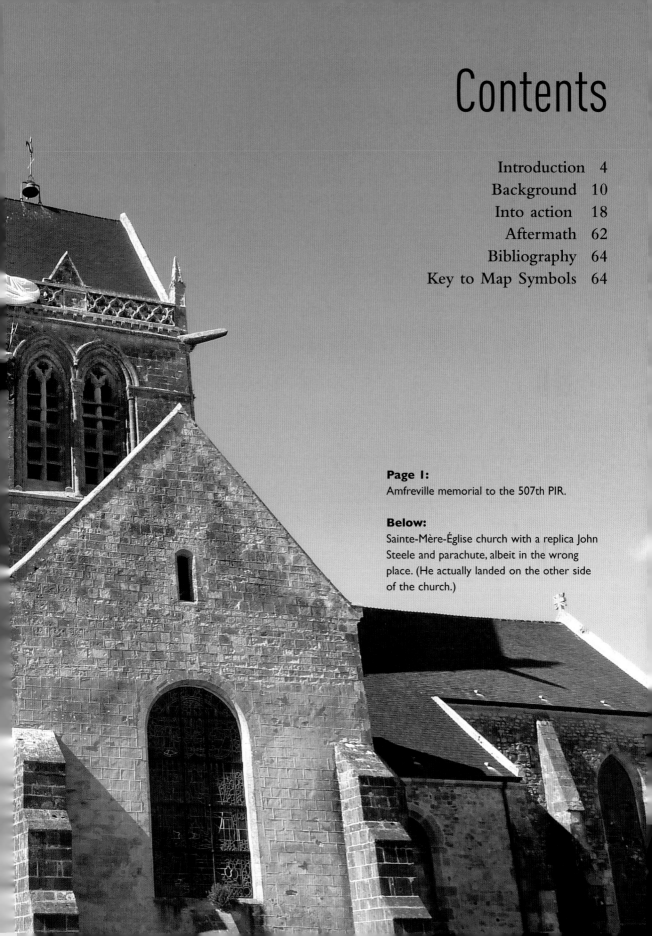

Contents

Page 1:
Amfreville memorial to the 507th PIR.

Below:
Sainte-Mère-Église church with a replica John Steele and parachute, albeit in the wrong place. (He actually landed on the other side of the church.)

Introduction

Operation Overlord was doubtless the most meticulously planned military assault of all time, and the longest in gestation. The Americans had wanted a cross-Channel attack as early as 1942, but had been persuaded to first test the Axis waters in North Africa. They had wanted it again in 1943, but cooler heads advised them to attack Sicily, and then Italy, instead.

Keeping the Allied armies occupied in the Mediterranean during those years may have played to Berlin's game, giving the Germans time to win their war in Russia—or not. But by late spring of 1944 both sides knew that the great Anglo-American invasion of France was finally coming. It would be the key to the war. If defeated, the English-speaking Allies would dare not try it again; if it succeeded, Germany would be caught between two fires, East and West, with no escape from ruin.

From the start, Allied planners counted on employing their elite airborne divisions—a surprise cudgel that could penetrate, disrupt, or at least confuse the German defenses before their main forces hit the beaches.

Nevertheless, there was still trepidation about the losses the airborne troops would incur. The Germans had proved unable to stop constant bomber streams from overflying their occupied territory; neither were they capable of stopping a 5,000-ship naval fleet. But lightly armed companies or battalions of paratroopers dropping within their own lines? These could be handled.

The Germans, after all, had written the book on airborne warfare, which the Allies had sought to copy. In May 1940 a few dozen glider-borne troops had neutralized the mighty Belgian fortress of Eban Emael, thus jumpstarting the initial Allied debacle in the West. In May

1941, German paratroops and air-landed battalions achieved the greatest strategic victory in the history of airborne, when they assaulted and conquered the island of Crete. This achievement spurred the Allies to accelerate the creation of their own airborne capability, while unbeknownst to them, Crete had signaled to Hitler that the days of large-scale airborne attacks were over. It wasn't simply the 4,500 casualties incurred on Crete—it was the fact that the first wave had dropped into a charnel-house, entire companies wiped out to a man upon landing. The ghastly evidence of the para-drop slaughter remained a feature of the Cretan landscape for weeks after the battle.

Allied planners naturally wondered whether the Germans, having pioneered airborne assaults, had also now become the experts in defending them. British Air Marshal Leigh-Mallory warned Dwight Eisenhower of a potential massacre of the US airborne. Certainly the previous record of Allied airborne drops provided mixed reasons for confidence. In the Mediterranean there had been a number of deadly miscues as well as mass confusion. The good news was that once on the ground, the hard-trained, volunteer paratroopers turned out to be the most ferocious fighters on either side. Ike kept to his original plan to thrust the airborne divisions into the midst of the German defenses in Normandy, in the dark hours prior to the seaborne assault on D-Day.

Specifically, while the British 6th Airborne Division seized objectives toward Caen, the two American divisions—the 82nd and 101st Airborne—would drop behind the German defenses at Utah Beach. They would simultaneously block German reinforcements from reaching the beach, while seizing bridges to allow

The Airborne Assault
June 6, 1944

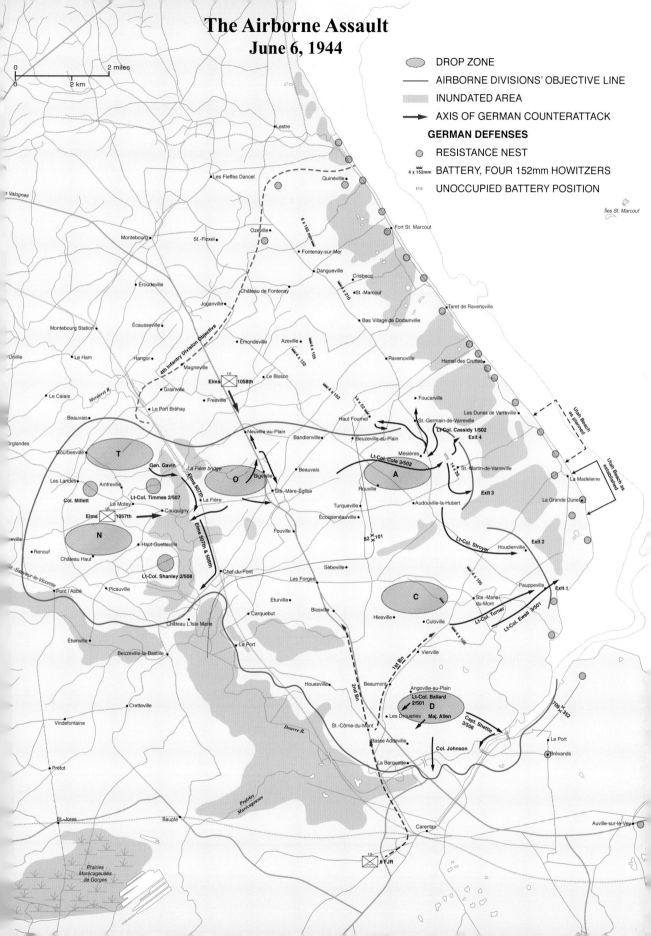

Legend:
- DROP ZONE
- AIRBORNE DIVISIONS' OBJECTIVE LINE
- INUNDATED AREA
- AXIS OF GERMAN COUNTERATTACK

GERMAN DEFENSES
- RESISTANCE NEST
- 4 x 152mm BATTERY, FOUR 152mm HOWITZERS
- UNOCCUPIED BATTERY POSITION

Scale: 0 — 2 miles / 0 — 2 km

Îles St. Marcouf

main-force US incursion inland. A focal point of American strategy was to saw off the Cotentin Peninsula as soon as possible, thus opening up the great port of Cherbourg to allow for rapid resupply of the invasion.

The 101st would be dropped immediately behind Utah and successively point south toward the town of Carentan, which sat astride the dividing line between the US Utah and Omaha beaches. The 82nd Airborne would be dropped farther inland, to get a headstart on US forces cutting off the peninsula. Originally the 82nd was tasked to land around St. Sauveur-le-Vicomte, some twenty miles inland. It wasn't till late May that Allied intelligence learned an entire new German division—the 91st Luftlande—had set up headquarters there. And German crews were erecting anti-glider poles, often topped with mines, all over the area. 82nd Airborne's assistant commander, Gen. James Gavin, wondered if the Allies' secret plan for the invasion had been betrayed.

The 82nd's mission was hastily switched—its three parachute infantry regiments (PIRs) would now drop on either side of the Merderet River, some seven miles from Utah. The 505th PIR would seize the crossroads town of Sainte-Mère-Église, and secure the near sides of two bridges across the Merderet. The 507th and 508th PIRs would drop on the far side of the river and secure the other ends of the bridges. Glider troops would arrive to reinforce. Together they would hold off German reinforcements from counterattacking the crucial beachhead.

Of course it is an axiom of war that no battle plan survives the first shot fired. An irony of D-Day is that the huge US landing on Utah proved to be a cakewalk—197 casualties in all—while the 82nd Airborne suffered 1,259 trying to keep the Germans away from it. By the time the 82nd was through in Normandy it had suffered several thousand more, continuing at the cutting edge of the offensive. In that kaleidoscope of battle the 82nd more than vindicated Ike's confidence in placing them at the forefront of the invasion.

ORDER OF BATTLE OF 82nd AIRBORNE DIVISION

Division commander: Major General Matthew B. Ridgway

Asst CO: Brigadier General James M. Gavin

82nd AB Div HQ Co

505th PIR (Col William E. Ekman): HQ and Service Co; 3 x Bn each of HQ Co and three Cos (1st: A, B, C; 2nd: D, E, F; 3rd: G, H, I Cos)

507th PIR (Col George V. Millett): HQ and Service Co; 3 x Bn each of HQ Co and three Cos (1st: A, B, C; 2nd: D, E, F; 3rd: G, H, I Cos)

508th PIR (Col Roy E. Lindquist): HQ and Service Co; 3 x Bn each of HQ Co and three Cos (1st: A, B, C; 2nd: D, E, F; 3rd: G, H, I Cos)

325th GIR (Col Harry L. Lewis): HQ and Service Co; 3 x Bn each of HQ Co and three Cos (1st: A, B, C; 2nd: D, E, F; 3rd: G, H, I Cos)

307th AB Engr Pl (Lt Col Robert S. Palmer); HQ C and A to C Cs

456th Para Fd Arty Bn (Lt Col Wagner J. d'Alessio): HQ Bty and A to D Btys

319th Glider Fd Arty Bn (Lt Col James C. Todd): HQ Bty and A to D Btys

320th Glider Fd Arty Bn (Lt Col Paul E. Wright): HQ Bty and A to D Btys

80th AB AAA Bn (Col Francis A. March): HQ Bty and A to F Btys

82nd AB Sigs Co (1Lt Robert B. Nerf)
307th AB Med Co (Maj William H. Houston)
82nd Airborne MP Pl (Maj Frederick G. McCollum)
782nd AB Ord Co
407th AB QM Co
82nd Div Recon Pl
82nd Div Pathfinder Gp
82nd Parachute Maintenance Co

Battle Casualties

The 82nd Airborne suffered 4,840 losses fighting in Normandy, or 46% of its strength (1,161 killed, 2,959 wounded, and 720 missing). The percentage of losses was naturally higher in the frontline paratroop and glider units. The 82nd's losses on D-Day alone were calculated at 1,259 dead, wounded, and missing. By the time the division was withdrawn from Normandy after 33 days of combat, it had lost 16 of its original 21 regimental and battalion commanders.

Above:
Sainte-Mère-Église Airborne Museum boasts a Waco room, a C-47 room, and this M4A4 75mm Sherman which replaced in 2017 the anachronistic Canadian-built M4A1E8 76mm that had been there before.

Right:
Iron Mike at La Fière. The Airborne Trooper Statue is a replica of the 1861 Leah Hiebert original modeled on Sgt. Major Runyon at Fort Bragg.

Opposite:
The area today, highlighting the major memorials and sites. Note also St.-Sauveur-le-Vicomte and La Haye-du-Puits, important locations for the fighting in the weeks after D-Day.

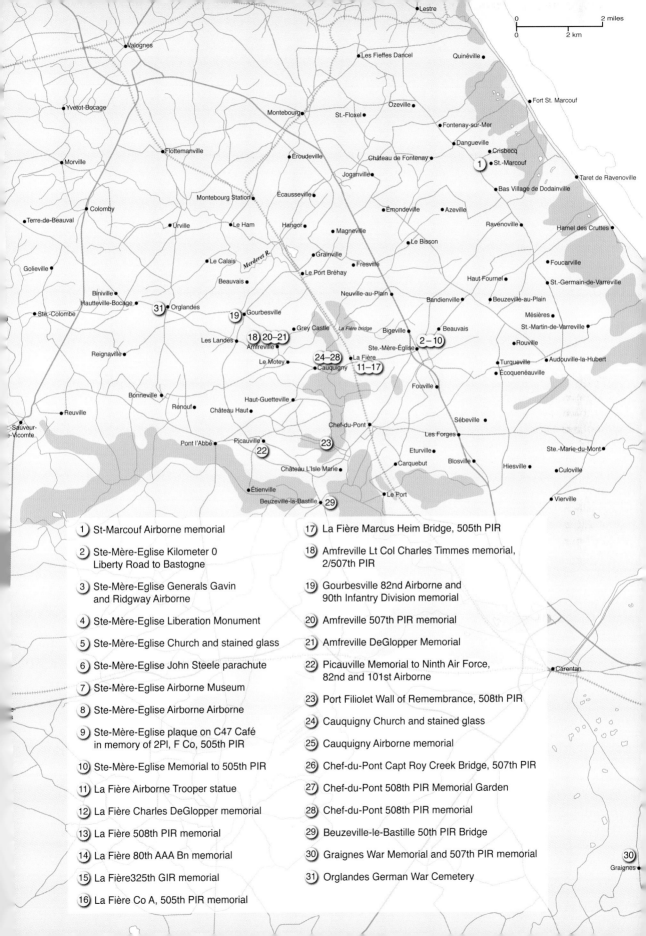

Lestre

Valognes

Les Fieffes Dancel

Quinéville

Fort St. Marcouf

Yvetot-Bocage

Montebourg

Ozeville

Fontenay-sur-Mer

St.-Floxel

Dangueville

Crisbecq

St.-Marcouf

Morville

Flottemanville

Éroudeville

Château de Fontenay

Taret de Ravenoville

Joganville

Bas Village de Dodainville

Montebourg Station

Écausseville

Émondeville

Azeville

Colomby

Urville

Le Ham

Hangor

Magneville

Ravenoville

Hamel des Cruttes

Le Bisson

Terre-de-Beauval

Grainville

Foucarville

Le Calais

Merderet R.

Fresville

Golleville

Le Port Bréhay

Haut Fournel

St.-Germain-de-Varreville

Beauvais

Neuville-au-Plain

Bandienville

Beuzeville-au-Plain

Biniville

Mésières

Hautteville-Bocage

31 Orglandes

19 Gourbesville

Grey Castle

La Fière bridge

Bigeville

St.-Martin-de-Varreville

Ste.-Colombe

18 20–21

Les Landes

Amfreville

Beauvais

2–10

Rouville

Ste.-Mère-Église

Reignaville

Le Motey

24–28

La Fière

Cauquigny

11–17

Turqueville

Audouville-la-Hubert

Écoquenéauville

Fouville

Bonneville

Haut-Guetteville

Renouf

Château Haut

Reuville

Chef-du-Pont

Sébeville

-Sauveur-
-Vicomte

Les Forges

Pont l'Abbé

Picauville

23

Eturville

Ste.-Marie-du-Mont

22

Château L'Isle Marie

Carquebut

Blosville

Hiesville

Culoville

Étienville

Le Port

Vierville

Beuzeville-la-Bastille

29

Carentan

① St-Marcouf Airborne memorial

② Ste-Mère-Eglise Kilometer 0
Liberty Road to Bastogne

③ Ste-Mère-Eglise Generals Gavin
and Ridgway Airborne

④ Ste-Mère-Eglise Liberation Monument

⑤ Ste-Mère-Eglise Church and stained glass

⑥ Ste-Mère-Eglise John Steele parachute

⑦ Ste-Mère-Eglise Airborne Museum

⑧ Ste-Mère-Eglise Airborne Airborne

⑨ Ste-Mère-Eglise plaque on C47 Café
in memory of 2Pl, F Co, 505th PIR

⑩ Ste-Mère-Eglise Memorial to 505th PIR

⑪ La Fière Airborne Trooper statue

⑫ La Fière Charles DeGlopper memorial

⑬ La Fière 508th PIR memorial

⑭ La Fière 80th AAA Bn memorial

⑮ La Fière325th GIR memorial

⑯ La Fière Co A, 505th PIR memorial

⑰ La Fière Marcus Heim Bridge, 505th PIR

⑱ Amfreville Lt Col Charles Timmes memorial,
2/507th PIR

⑲ Gourbesville 82nd Airborne and
90th Infantry Division memorial

⑳ Amfreville 507th PIR memorial

㉑ Amfreville DeGlopper Memorial

㉒ Picauville Memorial to Ninth Air Force,
82nd and 101st Airborne

㉓ Port Filiolet Wall of Remembrance, 508th PIR

㉔ Cauquigny Church and stained glass

㉕ Cauquigny Airborne memorial

㉖ Chef-du-Pont Capt Roy Creek Bridge, 507th PIR

㉗ Chef-du-Pont 508th PIR Memorial Garden

㉘ Chef-du-Pont 508th PIR memorial

㉙ Beuzeville-le-Bastille 50th PIR Bridge

㉚ Graignes War Memorial and 507th PIR memorial

㉛ Orglandes German War Cemetery

30

Graignes

0   2 miles
0   2 km

Background

Opposite, Above:
Training at Camp Toccoa, GA. Paratroopers were drilled to become the fittest soldiers in the US Army.

Opposite, Below:
Inside a CG-4 Waco glider. Nearly 14,000 were built during the war and the Air Mobility Command Museum, Dover AFB, DE identifies its carrying as 13 troops, or cargo loads that could include a Jeep with a crew of four plus equipment, or a 75mm howitzer with its guncrew of three, ammunition, and supplies.

The 82nd Infantry Division was formed shortly after America's entry into the Great War, and achieved a stellar combat record, from the St. Mihiel Offensive to the Meuse-Argonne, where it produced perhaps the most famous US soldier of the war, Sgt. Alvin York.

The 82nd was quickly reactivated after Pearl Harbor, initially under the command of Maj. Gen. Omar Bradley. That summer of 1942, on evidence the Germans had shown about the potential of airborne warfare, the Americans sought to create an airborne arm of their own, and the 82nd (along with the 101st Div) was singled out. Bradley was promoted to higher command and the division's new commander became Matthew Ridgway. His artillery officer was Maxwell Taylor, and one of his young officers was West Pointer James Gavin.

Initially the division consisted of one paratrooper regiment (the 504th) and three glider ones, but that ratio was changed to two paratroop regiments (the 505th being added) and one glider (the 325th). While glidermen could be assigned from the regular infantry, the US Army realized that paratroopers needed to be volunteers, and so the call went out to active young men who wished the most daring job in the service.

Though German propaganda liked to portray US paratroopers as "Chicago gangsters," the reality was that they were more likely to be Oklahoma or Alabama farmboys, which was worse. Kids of the Depression, with high school education at best, they were raised on tales of their Confederate or Indian-fighting forebears, and to many the army meant the first real income they'd seen, plus their first chance at being considered elite.

The 82nd Airborne's home base was at Fort Bragg, North Carolina, where the troopers were put through the most rigorous training in the entire US Army. Physical hardihood as well as weapons proficiency were stressed. Most of the young men had never been on a plane prior to being tasked with jumping out of one. Justifiably, those who survived the brutal training came to see themselves as a notch above normal infantry. The true test would come in combat, however, and the 82nd Airborne wouldn't have long to wait.

In April 1943, with the fight in North Africa still raging, the 82nd AB sailed from New York aboard the converted troop ship USS *Monterrey*. En route, to keep secrecy, they had to strip off their divisional insignia and untuck their pants from their jump boots so they would appear as regular infantry. Thus there was surprise when they disembarked at Casablanca on May 10 to be greeted by a band on the dock playing "Johnny the Jumper the Parachute Man." But the 82nd had missed the main fighting.

The division moved by truck and rail to near the Algerian border, next to a French airfield. Here their training resumed, though more disagreeable than ever with intense heat, flies, scorpions, and hard, rocky ground that caused jump injuries. An additional problem were the impoverished locals, who would steal everything not nailed down. At the beginning of July, as the Allied invasion of Sicily neared, the 82nd flew to a staging ground in Tunisia, closer to Mediterranean breezes.

Operation Husky, the invasion of Sicily, set the pattern that would be followed at Normandy, with bombing to soften up the defenses, airborne troops dropped behind the beachheads, naval gunfire plastering the beaches themselves, and then a huge amphibious delivery of ground forces. But there were still kinks to be worked out, especially with the airborne element.

On the night of July 9–10, 1943, the sea-breezes became 40mph headwinds which played murderous havoc with the paratroopers—initially the 505th PIR with a battalion of the 504th and support units. On that dark, windy night hardly any paratroopers hit their designated DZs. Yet for the first time the 82nd AB was able to demonstrate its pure combat skill. In small units the troopers proved aggressive and their wide dispersal caused confusion as well as heavy losses in the Axis rear.

It was in Sicily that the 505th PIR's commander, James Gavin, began to found his legend. The first man out of his plane, "Jumpin' Jim" fought his way through the Sicilian countryside, gradually gathering troops around him as he marched to the sound of the guns. He set up shop on Biazza Ridge, the key ground between the vulnerable US beachhead and the oncoming Hermann Goering Panzer Division, and held off the panzers long enough for the US 1st and 45th divisions to gain their footing.

Gavin's heroics aside, the big airborne problem with Sicily came when the 82nd AB's second wave arrived on the night of July 11. By now the US fleet was offshore, and had been attacked by the Luftwaffe all day. When 177 C-47s carrying the rest of the 504th PIR overflew the fleet that night, a nervous gunner mistook the looming shapes for enemy bombers and opened fire. AA gunners on the rest of the fleet and shore followed likewise, and 23 paratrooper-laden planes were shot down, 37 others damaged. Eight simply turned back with their human cargo while others returned to base with blood-soaked fuselages. For the US it was the worst friendly-fire incident of the war and caused a rethinking of airborne doctrine.

The invasion of Italy came too quickly, though, for the combat value of the 82nd AB to be neglected. After a harebrained scheme to drop the division on Rome was dismissed—at the last minute, even as some paras were boarding their planes—the main US invasion ran into trouble. The Germans were practically waiting for them at Salerno, and the invasion force ran into a buzzsaw of fire. The whole enterprise was in danger of failure until the 504th PIR was dropped behind the German right to seize a key height, while the 505th was dropped on the beachhead itself to bolster the wavering front. After a few days of the battle hanging in abeyance the Germans finally cried uncle and the Allies had their lodgment.

A further consequence of Salerno—one that would plague US airborne forces for the rest of the war—was that once seeing the combat capability of the paratroopers, ground-force commanders hated to let them go. While the 505th PIR and other 82nd units withdrew to the UK to prepare for the invasion of France, Gen. Mark Clark requested that the 504th stay with him in Italy. Col. Tucker's troopers thus became the spearhead of Fifth Army through its tough mountain battles, and during its invasion at Anzio. It would be five months before the 504th could rejoin its division, and only then after horrific losses. This also meant that in Operation Overlord, the 505th PIR would be the only combat-experienced paratrooper regiment in the Allied order of battle.

After a rest in Sicily and then a roundabout sail through the Atlantic (to avoid U-boats) the bulk of the 82nd AB set up bivouac in Northern Ireland. Just in time for winter, troopers' accounts invariably record the switch from the Mediterranean as unpleasant. But in February they were moved to England, through Liverpool, and set up comfortable camps in the Midlands. Their tents had solid floors, plus stoves, and there were also the charms of the English countryside and people to enjoy—and the pubs (taverns).

To replace the hard-fighting 504th PIR, the 82nd Airborne was given the 507th and 508th PIRs, new untested outfits. Its glider regiment, the 325th, was

Opposite:
A C-47—the military version of the DC-3—showing under-fuselage equipment containers.

Left:
Men of the 504th PIR, 82nd Airborne, in Sicily.

Below left:
In North Africa before Husky; note 1943 equipment.

Below:
82nd AB commander Matthew Ridgway (center) in Sicily, July 25, 1943.

Left:

On November 18, 1943, 505th PIR sailed to Northern Ireland on the USAT (US Attack Transport) *Frederick Funston* in a convoy with ships bearing other 82nd Airborne units (325th GIR was aboard *James O'Hara*.) They were joined by the 507th who arrived on December 5 aboard HMS *Strathnaver* and the 508th on January 9, 1944, on USAT *James Parker*. The Portstewart war memorial has a plaque remembering the 508th's sojourn in nearby Camp Cormore, January 9–March 11, 1944.

Center left:

Another Irish memorial, this one at Killymoon Castle, Cookstown, is dedicated to the men of the 505th Regimental Combat Team who were stationed in there December 9, 1943–February 13, 1944. *courtesy Andy Glenfield/ww2ni.webs.com*

Below and Detail:

In front of Wollaton Hall in Nottingham stands a monument commemorating the 508th PIR's wartime camp there.

Opposite:

1 and 2 Many 82nd units moved to the county of Leicestershire in England in spring 1944. The 505th PIR camped in Quorn and returned after fighting in Normandy. These memorials are in Quorn's Stafford Orchard Park in front of an avenue of trees planted in May 1952.

3 and 4 The Curzon Arms pub in Quorn was a regular haunt for the 505th PIR who were camped on the Farnham estate at Quorn House.

given the 2/401st from the 101st AB, to build it up to three battalions instead of two. While the 505th PIR was quartered near Leicester, the 507th and 508th were stationed on elegant estates outside Nottingham.

Since the 505th was the only combat-experienced PIR, its commander, Jim Gavin, was promoted to the task of standardizing tactics throughout the US airborne, including among the 101st AB. This would prove invaluable in Normandy, once many of the paratroopers became accidentally mixed.

As spring came to Britain the training intensified. New volunteers were absorbed and weak-links weeded out. The 504th PIR finally got back from Italy but had suffered so many casualties it wasn't considered combat-ready. Nevertheless some 50 of its troopers volunteered to serve as pathfinders on D-Day. Gavin, as well as division commander Matthew Ridgway, was determined that the 82nd would be honed to a fine edge. As D-Day neared, officers down to platoon level underwent map exercises, and in the final days were assigned their exact objectives. The wisest advice, however, was issued by a British brigadier of the 3rd Paras when he stated, "Gentlemen, don't be surprised if chaos reigns; it undoubtedly will."

1 and 2 504th PIR was encamped in what is today called the Arboretum beside St. Denys Church in Evington, just outside Leicester. They regularly worshipped in the church and left their colors there. A modern flag was handed over in 2005.

3 Memorial in the northeast of Leicester's Victoria Park in tribute to the men of 82nd Airborne.

4 Memorial to the 325th GIR and 504th PIR who camped in Scraptoft and Evington, Leicestershire.

5 Buildup to D-Day—Waco gliders are assembled from their shipping containers.

6 Spanhoe airfield came under the aegis of US Ninth Air Force. The 315th Troop Carrier Group arrived there on February 7, 1944, operating the C-47 Skytrain and the C-53 Skytrooper. Four Troop Carrier Squadrons would use Spanhoe—the 34th, 43rd, 309th, and 310th—all dropping paras on D-Day.

7 Saltby airfield was used by the RAF and the USAAF. C-47s of 314th Troop Carrier Group dropped 82nd Airborne on D-Day and would go on to drop British 1st Airborne Division during Operation Market Garden.

Into action

Below:
Glidermen wearing Mae Wests on their way to boarding.

Opposite, Above:
On display at the Air Mobility Command Museum in Dover AFB, DE, the "Turf & Sport Special" was rescued in 1986. Its markings are those of the 61st Troop Carrier Squadron, which it wore on the night of D-Day.

Opposite, Below:
Waiting to board a Horsa glider. Aside from the hastily painted recognition stripes—a last-minute initiative to prevent Sicily-type friendly-fire incidents—note the quick attempt to cover over the RAF roundel with a USAAF star.

Just before midnight ushered in June 6, 1944, 377 C-47s roared to life on airfields across southern England. The 82nd Airborne was finally on its way to spearhead the greatest invasion in history. The lesson of Sicily learned, the US flight plan avoided the Allied fleet in the Channel, instead coming in over the west coast of the Cotentin Peninsula. The British had set up a floating beacon off Guernsey to guide the pilots to their turning-point, and this they did. But then directly over the target area in Normandy was a cloud bank. It was a fluke accumulation that the weather people couldn't have predicted. The lead serial, carrying the 2/505, jumped over the bank, and the pilots, assisted by accurately dropped pathfinders, put on their green lights right over target. They were going a bit too high, too fast, but at least the 2/505 and the 1/505 landed on or near their drop zone. They were about the only ones.

The following formations flew straight through the clouds, and pilots naturally began spreading out in the soup. By now German AA fire was also streaming up, and pilots either swerved or ducked to avoid it. The rest of the pathfinder teams had either been misdropped or couldn't light up because Germans were on their DZs. The pilots couldn't see the ground below, and had to observe radio silence; meantime all they knew was they weren't allowed to carry any paratroopers back to England. A few pilots circled back through German fire to make sure, while others just put on their green jump-lights while they could.

The result was that, while the lead 505th PIR landed with fair accuracy, the 507th and especially the 508th became scattered to the winds. Half their men landed on the wrong side of the Merderet, while half of the rest became lost to their units.

In addition to the problems of the pilots, there were two other issues for the paratroopers, which Allied intelligence should have solved. First, after all the months of reconnaissance, no one had realized that the Germans had created vast flooded areas around the Merderet and Douve rivers. With grass and weeds growing up through the swamps, Allied aerial recon hadn't recognized the water, and only anticipated "soft ground." A number of heavily laden paratroopers drowned after falling into the flooded areas. And even if a man could usually wade out of the swamps, they were doom to any equipment bundle that fell in. Much of the careful plan to equip the 82nd with radios, heavy weapons, and ammo was lost in the marshes.

Below:

Horsa gliders being made ready for D-Day.

Opposite, Above and Below:

Equipment checks prior to boarding. Men would have to assist each other to don as much gear as they could carry as well as secure the straps. Lower image shows the 508th PIR prior to D-Day.

The second intelligence surprise was that somehow the true nature of Normandy's hedgerows had failed to filter down to the Americans. Aerial recon indeed showed hedges dividing fields. These were not unusual in America and commonplace on training grounds in England, never a huge obstacle. But the French hedgerows (*bocage*) were different—veritable walls built up over centuries, of packed stone, earth, and roots, with foliage up to 30 feet high. The Americans had expected bushes; instead they fell into a labyrinth.

Of all the misdrops in the dark early hours of June 6, the ones on Sainte-Mère-Église were the most spectacular. Intended to land outside the town, two or three sticks—at least 30 men—came floating down right on top of it. A house had earlier caught fire from a bomb or flare, so that at two in the morning the citizens as well as the German garrison (an AA support company) were all in the streets, with a fully illuminated sky when US paratroopers began floating in. It was a surreal scene.

The Germans opened fire on the intruders, two of whom fell into the burning house itself and whatever grenades or mortar ammo they were carrying exploded. Other paratroopers landed in the streets or got hung up on trees and were shot, their bodies remaining for another day. Two men landed on the town's church steeple and one just dangled there. A German posted inside the steeple was unsure what to do about the visitor outside his window, but finally pulled a knife to saw off his strings so he could climb down.

A couple hours later Ed Krause's 3/505 entered Sainte-Mère-Église, killing 11 Germans and taking 30 prisoner. Krause had brought along the American flag that the 82nd AB had first raised over Naples, and now he raised it again over Sainte-Mère-Église, the first French town to be liberated by the Americans in the invasion.

The 2/505's Col. Vandervoort had broken his ankle on the drop, but had commandeered a French cart with a couple of troopers to steer him around. He spent the

Continued on page 24

Above:
About half the 82nd's 57mm guns on D-Day were lost in marshes or crashes, but the ones that survived the glider journey proved invaluable.

Above right:
Inside a CG-4A Waco glider (in British service they were dubbed "Hadrians").

Below:
Boarding on June 5. A paratrooper stick usually consisted of about 18 men.

Right:
OK, it's well known but sums it all up brilliantly. Joseph Gorenc of 506th PIR. Many troopers ended up carrying as much as their own weight in weapons and gear, and had to be pushed and pulled by others to board an aircraft.

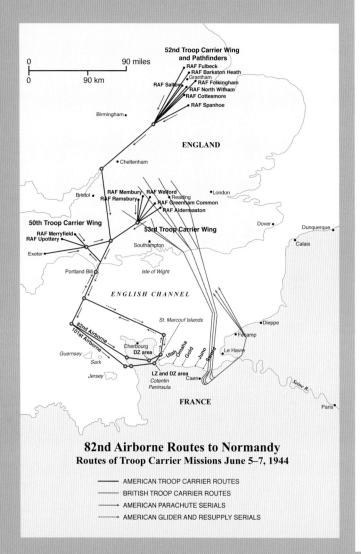

82nd Airborne Routes to Normandy
Routes of Troop Carrier Missions June 5–7, 1944

——— AMERICAN TROOP CARRIER ROUTES
——— BRITISH TROOP CARRIER ROUTES
------> AMERICAN PARACHUTE SERIALS
------> AMERICAN GLIDER AND RESUPPLY SERIALS

dark hours assembling his battalion, until at daylight he had about 400 men. (Many of these were 507th and 508th troopers, plus some lost Screaming Eagles.) Then he headed to his original objective, Neuville-au-Plain, a hamlet north of the town, to provide flank support for the 82nd's main thrust toward the Merderet. Halfway there, however, he was ordered back to Sainte-Mère-Église, which had come under a strong counterattack from the south. Vandervoort complied, but had the presence of mind to leave a platoon under a tough, half-Cherokee captain, Turner Turnbull, in place against a possible German counterattack from the north.

As daylight on D-Day broke, Turnbull's 40-some men spotted a long column of enemy troops marching down the Cherbourg highway against them. Oddly, they were in nonchalant formation and singing. A few bursts from US machine-gun fire put them to ground, however, and the "hi-ho" ended as German squads began shifting off to left and right to flank the American fireblock. Vandervoort personally came forward to give Turnbull a 57mm gun found in a crashed glider, and this turned out handy as the German infantry had an SPG following up their assault. In the end the US gun was knocked out, but so was the StuG, until in late afternoon, Turnbull pulled his last-standing 16 men back

Continued on page 32

MISSION BOSTON (Paras D-Day)
RAF Fulbeck (45 C-47s; 1/507th PIR)
RAF Barkston Heath (72 C-47s; 2/and 3/507th PIR)
RAF Folkingham (72 C-47s; 1/and 3/508th PIR)
RAF North Witham (9 C-47s; Pathfinders)
RAF Saltby (60 C-47s; HQ and 2/508th PIR; B/307th AB Engr Bn)
RAF Cottesmore (72 C-47s; 2/and 3/505th PIR; elements of 456th Para Fd Arty)
RAF Spanhoe (48 C-47s; Div HQ; 1/ and HHC/505th PIR

MISSION DETROIT (Gliders dawn D-Day)
RAF Ramsbury (52 C-47s; 82nd AB Div HQ, 82nd AB Sig Co, A/ and B/80th AB AAA Bn, 82nd AB Div Arty)

MISSION ELMIRA (Gliders dusk D-Day)
RAF Membury (50 C-47s; 319th G FA Bn, 307th AB

Med Co, A/307th AB Engr Bn, 82nd AB Div Arty)
RAF Ramsbury (26 C-47s; C/HQ 80th AAA Bn, 82nd AB Div Arty, 82nd AB Sig Co)
RAF Welford (50 C-47s; 320th G FA Bn)
RAF Greenham Common (50 C-47s; 82nd AB Recon Pl, 82nd AB Sig Co, 82nd AB Div HQ, 307th AB Engr Bn)

MISSION GALVESTON (Gliders dawn D+1)
RAF Ramsbury (50 C-47s 1/325th GIR, A/307th AB Engr Bn)
RAF Aldermaston (50 C-47s; HQ/ and HQ Co/325th GIR, A/307th AB Engr Bn, 82nd AB Recon Pl, 82nd AB Div Arty)

MISSION HACKENSACK (Gliders dawn D+1)
RAF Upottery (50 C-47s; 2/325th GIR, 2/401st GIR)
RAF Merryfield (50 C-47s; HQ 2/325th GIR, HQ 2/401st GIR, Service Co/325th GIR)

24

Left:
The 82nd and 101st ABs were routed to approach the Cotentin from the west so as not to overfly the Allied fleet.

Right:
The actual drop pattern on D-Day. Note the near absence of dots on every drop zone except "O" near Sainte-Mère-Église. DZ–O had been assigned to the 505th PIR, the only combat-experienced PIR in the invasion. The 505th's pathfinders were also the only ones to successfully reach and signal from their DZ.

Below right:
A few hours before their departure for Normandy, men of the 508th PIR receive the message of General Eisenhower addressed to all the troops participating in the invasion.

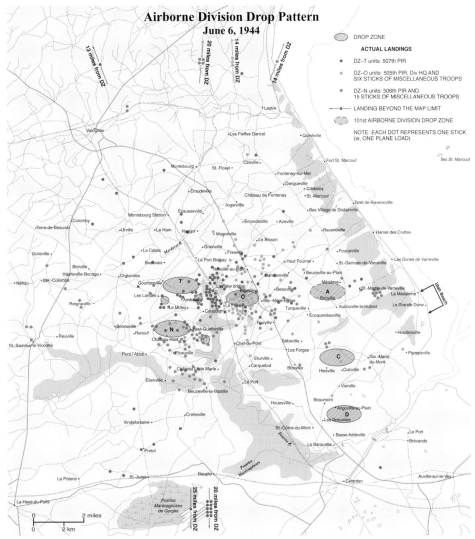

Airborne Division Drop Pattern
June 6, 1944

DROP ZONE

ACTUAL LANDINGS

- DZ–T units: 507th PIR
- DZ–O units: 505th PIR, Div HQ AND SIX STICKS OF MISCELLANEOUS TROOPS
- DZ–N units: 506th PIR AND 15 STICKS OF MISCELLANEOUS TROOPS
- LANDING BEYOND THE MAP LIMIT
- 101st AIRBORNE DIVISION DROP ZONE

NOTE: EACH DOT REPRESENTS ONE STICK (ie, ONE PLANE LOAD)

Mission Elmira consisted of 176 C-47s acting as glider tugs for 36 Waco and 140 Horsa gliders, divided into one serial of 26 and three serials of 50 tug-glider combinations. An additional C-47, which had returned to base earlier without dropping its stick of paratroopers, accompanied the flight. The planned and briefed landing zone for the gliders was LZ–W, some two miles southeast of Saint-Mère-Eglise. But Germans were still around it and frantic efforts were made to divert the landings to DZ–O. One of the results was mass confusion over the Contentin, as these photos attest.

Above left:
Wacos and their tugs coming in over the coast. Now that the Germans were awake, gliders were sent in from the east rather than west to reduce their exposure to AA fire.

Below left:
Jeeps and equipment leaving a LZ.

Above:
Lt. James A. Gayley and 16 of his men (Co. A, 325th GIR) killed in the crash of their glider near Hiesville on June 7. The plywood Horsas would shatter more easily than the smaller Waco gliders, which had metal framing.

Center right:
One of 36 troopers who drowned or were perhaps shot in the flooded areas.

Below right:
Chalk #2 of Serial 31, part of Elmira, landed on LZ–W at 21:20 on June 6 carrying nine soldiers. This successful landing was taken in stride by the first local residents on the scene. Mission Elmira was trailed from Greenham Common by the 438th TCG, it landed on the LZ–W (des Forges) at 21:20 on June 6 and carried nine soldiers from the 82nd Recon Pl.

Showing the dispersal of the drop, men of the 82nd joined units of the 101st AB at Ravenoville and St. Marcouf on the east coast of the Cotentin.

Left and Below:
Ravenoville, just behind Utah Beach, with the Eternal Heroes Memorial.

Right:
Saint Marcouf, also near Utah, was the site of a powerful German coastal battery that on D-Day succeeded in sinking a destroyer, the USS *Corry*.

Above and Opposite, above: Sainte-Mère-Église. In 1944 motor vehicles were rare in the town except for those of the opposing militaries. Then as now, however, the church and its square serves as the focal point of the village.

to Sainte-Mère-Église. The gallant Cherokee would soon be killed by a German shell, but his brave stand against the first enemy counterattack from the north would be remembered.

Jim Gavin jumped with the 508th PIR, and found himself alone on the west (far) side of the Merderet. His aide soon joined him, and together they assembled a fair body of fellow strays. A couple of gliders landed in the swamp nearby, and Gavin's ad hoc crew wasted time trying to wrest

a jeep and 57mm gun out of the wrecks. This proved fruitless while meantime Gavin identified the elevated rail line across the flooded area as the proper place to assemble. Indeed, during those dark early hours, the rail line became a magnet for misdropped paratroopers, because it was the one place they could identify from their maps and thus orient themselves. Gavin and his party waded across the swamp and set up a CP. To his consternation *Continued on page 47*

Continued on page 47

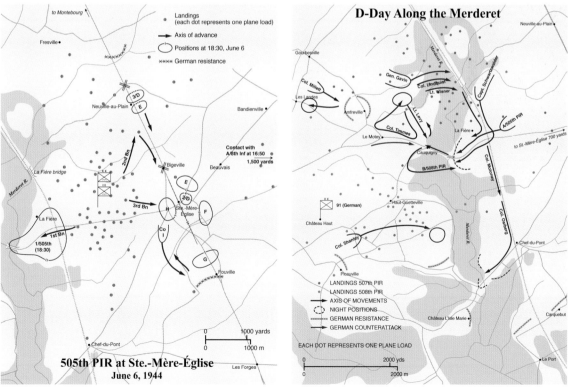

Landings
(each dot represents one plane load)

→ Axis of advance

⬭ Positions at 18:30, June 6

xxxx German resistance

to Montebourg

Fresville

Neuville-au-Plain

3/D

E

2nd Bn

Bigeville

La Fière bridge

XX
III

3rd Bn

La Fière

1st Bn

1/505th
(18:30)

H

Ste.-Mère-
Église

Co I

E

2/D

F

G

Fouville

Bandienville

Contact with
A/8th Inf at 16:50
1,500 yards

Beauvais

0   1000 yards
0   1000 m

Chef-du-Pont

Les Forges

505th PIR at Ste.-Mère-Église
June 6, 1944

D-Day Along the Merderet

Neuville-au-Plain

Gourbesville

Col. Millett

Les Landes

Amfreville

Le Motey

Col. Timmes

Gen. Gavin

Col. Lindquist

Lt. Wisner

Merderet R.

Capt. Schwartzwalder

La Fière

A/505th PIR

to St.-Mère-Église 700 yards

Lt. Levy

Cauquigny

B/508th PIR

Col. Maloney

Col. Ostberg

Merderet R.

XX
91 (German)

Château Haut

Haut-Guetteville

Chef-du-Pont

Col. Shanley

Picauville

Château L'Isle Marie

Carquebut

Le Port

● LANDINGS 507th PIR
● LANDINGS 508th PIR
→ AXIS OF MOVEMENTS
⬭ NIGHT POSITIONS
⬭ GERMAN RESISTANCE
→ GERMAN COUNTERATTACK

EACH DOT REPRESENTS ONE PLANE LOAD

0   2000 yds
0   2000 m

Sainte-Mère-Eglise today and in 1944, looking south.
La Fière, Chef du Pont, and the Merderet River are to
the right (west) of both photos.

Street scenes of Sainte-Mère-Église from June 1944 and today. Though many paratroopers complained about the amount of equipment they had to carry into Normandy, the soldier at right appears to have warmed to the task.

EN HOMMAGE
AUX GÉNÉRAUX RIDGWAY ET GAVIN
ET A TOUS LES VAILLANTS
LIBÉRATEURS DE NOTRE CITÉ

Ste MÈRE - ÉGLISE RECONNAISSANTE
JUIN 1944

IN GRATEFUL TRIBUTE
TO GENERALS RIDGWAY AND GAVIN
AND TO ALL THE GALLANT
LIBERATORS OF OUR TOWN

Ste MÈRE - ÉGLISE
JUNE 1944

GUERRE 1939-1944
EN HOMMAGE
AUX FRANÇAIS DE Ste MÈRE ÉGLISE
QUI ONT DONNÉ LEUR VIE
POUR RACHETER NOTRE LIBERTÉ

KmO
VOIE
DE LA
LIBERTÉ
1944

Opposite, Above:
The Carentan–Cherbourg highway north of Sainte-Mère-Église, looking back toward the town following the repulse of a German counterattack.

Opposite, Below:
Looking north toward Neuville-au-Plain, this StuG was knocked out by a glider-borne 57mm manned by the 505th PIR during the D-Day counter-assault by the 91st Luftlande Division.

Above:
Though the 82nd AB was not averse to employing captured enemy equipment, this German weapons carrier had seen better days.

Left:
A moment of relaxation in Sainte-Mère-Église as locals contemplate a temporary move to safety.

This spread:

Then-and-now scenes from Sainte-Mère-Église. Though many paratroopers commented on the cows in Normandy (Gen. Ridgway said his first encounter in France was with two dairy cows that scared him in the dark) there were horses in the countryside also, much to the delight of some troopers.

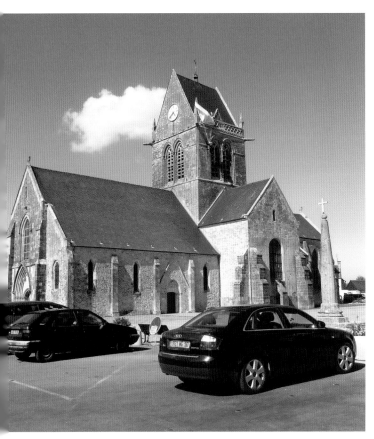

Opposite, Above, and Left:
The church in Sainte-Mère-Église. Note the parachute and effigy of paratrooper John Steele that is on the church today.

Opposite, Below left and right:
After the church's original glass was destroyed in the battle, the villagers commissioned new art, this time commemorating their liberation on D-Day. One scene depicts 82nd paratroopers on either side of the Madonna and Child; the other features the winged St. Michael, patron saint of paratroopers, with an inscription below: "To the memory of those who through their sacrifice liberated Sainte-Mère-Église."

Below left:
The John Steele Memorial at the Sainte-Mère-Église Airborne Museum.

Below right:
A monument on the market square to all the Allied airborne forces that participated on D-Day, along with their insignia and battle casualties. It is inscribed, "They gave their tomorrow for our today."

AIRBORNE

VERGERS "TIMMES"

En hommage
au Lt Colonel
Charles J. TIMMES
et à ses parachutistes
du 507th P.I.R

82ème Airborne Div.

6-9 juin 1944

Above and Left:

Monument commemorating the fierce battle waged by elements of the 507th and 508th PIRs that landed west of the River Merderet, and the 325th GIR that reinforced them. The site is dedicated to the commander of the 507th PIR, Lt. Col. Charles Timmes, who was dropped at 02:30 on D-Day, almost drowned in a drenched meadow near Amfreville, but for four days managed to maintain an ad hoc defense in an orchard among attacking Germans.

there were far more 507th and 508th men on the east side of the river than on the regiments' real objective—the west side. This vindicated his decision to come over to the east; nevertheless there were still troopers on west side who took initiatives of their own.

Col. Tom Shanley's 508th had been meant to seize Pont d'Abbe on the Douve River, and the nearby village of Picauville. But the Germans were there in strength so Shanley assembled what men he could on a map-point called Hill 30. This was not much of a height, as hedgerows and foliage interrupted sight in any direction, but that same factor obscured his men from the Germans. In fact, Hill 30 was a superb tactical point from which to intercept German counterattacks against the Merderet crossings.

Lt. Col. Timmes of the 2/507 assembled about 100 men. Finding his first object of Amfreville full of Germans, he set up shop in an orchard nearby, whereupon, like Shanley, he drew German attention and served as a breakwater against their counterattacks. Col. Millet, the 507th's commander, eventually assembled about

400 men of his own, but his attacks on Amfreville ran into superior forces and Millet himself was captured.

Fifty-two gliders had followed up the nocturnal para-drops but most of them crashed into hedgerows or water. More followed at daylight with equipment, and then another wave came at dusk on D-Day with part of the 325th GIR. But Germans still covered the drop-zones with fire, and losses were severe. Nevertheless, by the end of June 6 the 82nd had secured at least the east side of the Merderet.

At La Fière bridge an epic battle raged throughout D-Day and beyond. It was behind a manor consisting of a large house, barn, stable, and outbuildings, all constructed of stone, with walls and hedgerows nearby (shown well in the aerial view on pp.52–53). Only the evening before, a German platoon had taken up position at the manor, setting up machine-gun nests and sniper positions. It took all morning for the 1/505 and other troopers to reduce the position, but then it appeared as if the 82nd had taken the bridge, as well as its adjoining 700-yard-long causeway across the swamp.

Above:

The bridge over the Merderet and the Manoir de La Fière, in a modern photo that betrays the ferocity of the battle for this spot, which both the 82nd AB and 91st Luftlande Division were determined to hold. (See also aerial view, pp. 52–53.)

Opposite, Below left and right:
As with La Fière, Chef du Pont to the south was the scene of heavy fighting around a bridge over the Merderet. The position was held by elements of the 507th PIR under command of Captain Roy Creek—the new bridge is named after him—and the 508th PIR. Memorials to the bravery of the latter unit can be found on the roadside (**Right**) and in the 508th PIR Memorial Garden opposite (**Left**). There, three stones commemorate the unit, O. B. Hill—the founder of the 508th PIR Association—and Capt. Rex Combs whose idea the garden was,

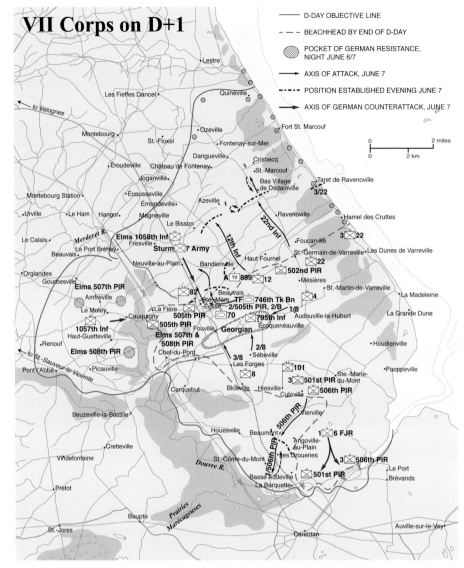

VII Corps on D+1

During the fight Gen. Gavin had arrived at the head of several hundred 507th and 508th men, but Major Kellam of the 1/505 told him the situation was in hand. Gavin went onward to Chef du Pont, some two miles south of La Fière, where there was another bridge and causeway across the Merderet. At Chef du Pont, Germans who tried to make a stand on the east side of the river were forced back through the village, but they brought up a gun on the far side of the causeway and began hammering in the American positions. By a stroke of luck, a US glider landed nearby with a 57mm gun, and the paras were able to

man it and knock out the German cannon. Nevertheless, several American attempts to storm the bridge were repulsed.

While the battle still raged at Chef du Pont, all went quiet at La Fière. The 1/505 held the bridge, and paras were also across the causeway at Cauquigny, a tiny hamlet consisting mainly of a bombed-out church. Cpt. Ben Schwartzwalder led some 40 507th men across the causeway from La Fière, where they had assisted in the fight for the manor. Declining to stay around Cauquigny, where nothing was then happening, he went onward in search of Timmes.

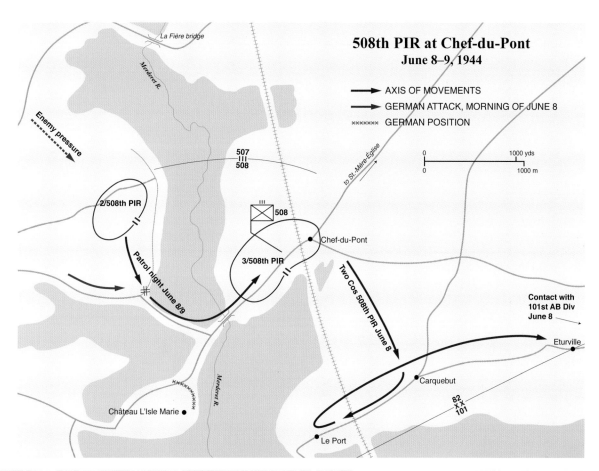

508th PIR at Chef-du-Pont
June 8–9, 1944

→ AXIS OF MOVEMENTS
→ GERMAN ATTACK, MORNING OF JUNE 8
✗✗✗✗✗✗✗ GERMAN POSITION

La Fière bridge

Merderet R.

Enemy pressure

507
508

to St.-Mère-Église

2/508th PIR

508

3/508th PIR

Patrol night June 8/9

Chef-du-Pont

Two Cos 508th PIR June 8

Contact with
101st AB Div
June 8

Eturville

Carquebut

82
101

Château L'Isle Marie

Merderet R.

Le Port

0   1000 yds
0   1000 m

It was midafternoon when the massive German counterattack began. It was the 1057th Regiment of the 91st Luftlande Division, supported by tanks (captured French Renaults) from the 100th Ersatz Abteilung. The Germans overran Cauquigny and poured onto the causeway toward La Fière bridge. Around the manor, the 1/505 braced itself. Company A had two-man bazooka teams on either side of the bridge's exit, plus a 57mm gun down the road. When the tanks got within range, the bazookamen rose up and methodically poured rocket rounds into the vehicles. The tanks evidently focused on the 57mm gun, which they knocked out, not seeing the deadly infantrymen at their feet. Though disabled, the lead tanks continued to pour fire into the American position, as did the following German infantry. The 1/505's commander, Maj. Kellam, rushed up to the bridge with more ammo but was killed, as was his XO. Finally the Germans pulled back to their side of the causeway, while their mortars and artillery continued to hammer the manor.

The next day the Germans attacked again with more tanks, and Company A of the 1/505, closest to the bridge, was shredded down to 14 men, nearly out of ammo. A trooper ran to Lt. John "Red Dog" Dolan asking if they should pull back. Dolan said no, and added in a note, "I don't know of a better place to die." Just minutes later it was the Germans who asked for a temporary truce in order to remove their wounded, and the relieved paratroopers granted it.

While the bridge at Chef du Pont finally fell to the 82nd, the Germans continued to make a main effort at La Fière. By now the 325th GIR was at hand, and on the night of June 8 its 1st Battalion was ordered to cross the swamp across a sunken road and hit the Germans from behind. The nocturnal attack turned into a fiasco amid successive ambushes, although one gliderman, Charles DeGlopper, earned a Medal of Honor when he singlehandedly held off a swarm of

Germans with his BAR long enough to allow the rest of his platoon to escape.

On the morning of June 9 the 3rd Battalion of the 325th Glider Infantry arrived at La Fière and was ordered to attack across the bridge and the long causeway. The 3/325's commander, Lt. Col. Carrell, declined to lead the attack and Gavin relieved him on the spot. To hedge his bet, Gavin went up to Captain Robert Rae, commanding a company of the 507th PIR, and told him that if the glidermen stalled on the causeway, Rae was to charge with his 90 paratroopers to stiffen them up. Gavin also arranged for the attack to be supported by the 90th Infantry Division's artillery, which had come within range from Utah Beach, plus a dozen Sherman tanks from the 746th Battalion, which had taken up a line behind the manor, plus every other mortar or machine gun in sight.

The attack began as planned, with the causeway and the opposite side of the flooded area, around Cauquigny, plastered with fire. An arranged smokescreen, however, failed to appear, or as one 505th trooper said, made as much smoke as a pack of Lucky Strikes. Glidermen began falling by the score, or taking cover in ditches alongside the causeway. Then the paras charged through and soon both the glidermen and paras had a toehold across the Merderet. Gavin himself came onto the causeway, as did Matthew Ridgway, while German fire still crisscrossed the area.

As daylight waned the Germans launched a ferocious counterattack against the 82nd's tenuous toehold, but it was their last gasp to hold the Merderet. The Americans held on, with the four-day battle for La Fière bridge having cost them a total of nearly 600 casualties.

Now that the Merderet bridges and causeways were clear, fresh troops, guns, and armor were able to flow in from Utah Beach. However, the 82nd Airborne was still needed to spearhead assaults inland, operations that were to prove as costly as the initial battles for the river.

Continued on page 58

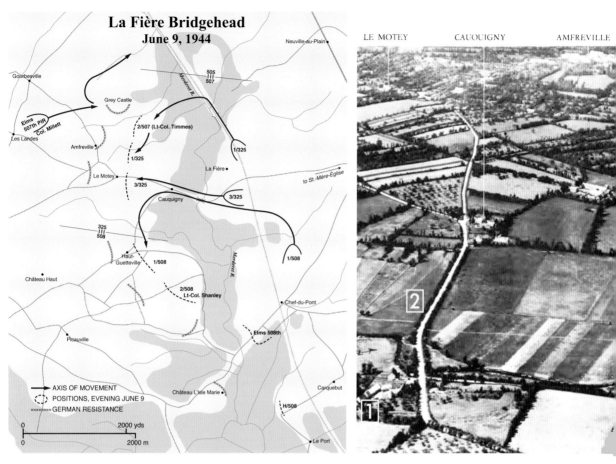

La Fière Bridgehead
June 9, 1944

Neuville-au-Plain

Gourbesville

Grey Castle

$\begin{array}{c}505\\ ||| \\ 507\end{array}$

Merderet R.

Elms
507th PIR
Col. Millett

Les Landes

2/507 (Lt.-Col. Timmes)

1/325

Amfreville

1/325

La Fière

to St.-Mère-Église

Le Motey

3/325

3/325

Cauquigny

$\begin{array}{c}325\\ ||| \\ 508\end{array}$

Merderet R.

1/508

Haut-
Guetteville

1/508

Château Haut

2/508
Lt.-Col. Shanley

Chef-du-Pont

Plseuville

Elms 508th

Carquebut

AXIS OF MOVEMENT
POSITIONS, EVENING JUNE 9
GERMAN RESISTANCE

Château L'Isle Marie

H/508

0   2000 yds
0   2000 m

Le Port

LE MOTEY   CAUQUIGNY   AMFREVILLE

2

1

Left:
Aerial view of the Manoir La Fière and its bridge. Remember the river would have been higher and the countryside to the left completely flooded during the battle. The 82nd's only way to cross was via a 750-yard-long causeway under German fire.

Inset, Far left:
Detail from the bronze table beside the Iron Mike statue showing bazooka action at the bridge.

Below:
If the 82nd found the La Fière causeway daunting, so did the Germans in their counterattacks across it. Here are three German tanks (captured Renaults) knocked out on the causeway just short of the bridge.

Opposite, Above:
The site of the causeway from Cauquigny (across from La Fière) today. This area was completely flooded on D-Day, though foliage peeking up from the water prevented Allied aerial recon from recognizing it.

Opposite, Below:
The restored church at Cauquigny along with its stained glass tribute to the 82nd AB and a memorial to the US airborne on the site.

Left and Below left:
The DeGlopper Memorial near Cauquigny, by the hedgerow where he singlehandedly held off a German attack—at the expense of his life—to allow time for his platoon to reach safety.

Left:
Lt. Kelso C. Horne of the 508th PIR on the way to St. Sauveur-le-Vicomte. He was subsequently wounded and while convalescing in England was as surprised as anyone to see his picture on the cover of *Life* magazine, August 14, 1944.

Right and Below:
St. Sauveur-le-Vicomte. By this time in the campaign the 82nd AB were no longer surprise shock troops. They were needed to spearhead the assaults of follow-up US infantry divisions.

Right, Below, and Bottom right
Street scenes in St. Sauveur-le-Vicomte, then and now. The town was bombed by US aircraft as well as hammered by artillery prior to the 82nd AB seizing it on the ground. Photo shows Co E, 505th and HQ Co, 2/505th PIR.

Opposite, Above:
The Filiolet Memorial Wall near Picauville, dedicated to the 508th PIR and featuring the names of 62 paratroopers, two pilots, and two French civilians killed during the battle.

On June 8 the 505th PIR was ordered to extend the Allied flank north of Sainte-Mère-Église, attacking north along the rail line with the 4th Div's 8th Regiment on its right and the 325th GIR on its left. It was tough hedgerow country, and the paratroopers frequently found themselves outpacing the other units. This not only put them in a perpetual salient, vulnerable to German flank attacks, but also subjected them to friendly fire, as supporting artillery didn't anticipate the speed of their advance. Nevertheless, by the 11th Neuville-au-Plain and Montebourg Station had fallen and were handed off to the 4th Division.

Across the Merderet, the rest of the 82nd drove west with the novice 90th Div in grueling battles that cost the 507th PIR alone 192 men in two days' fighting. German resistance stiffened with each step, behind hedgerows and from a commanding height called Hill 181, but the 82nd twisted itself into the town. In another case of advancing faster than expected, elements of the 505th PIR had no sooner crossed the Douve River when US fighter-bombers swooped in to bomb the bridge behind them. After taking the key town of St. Sauveur-le-Vicomte the 82nd handed off to the 9th Infantry Div, which two days later reached the sea to cut off the Cotentin Peninsula.

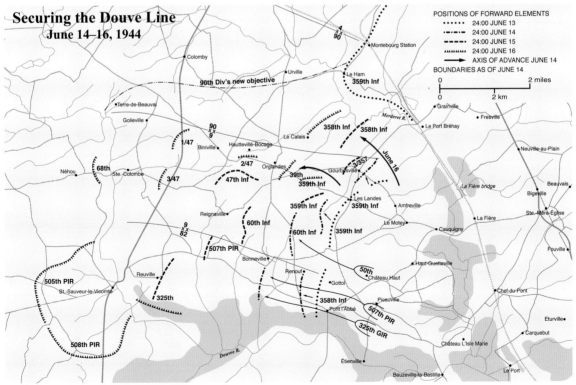

Securing the Douve Line
June 14–16, 1944

POSITIONS OF FORWARD ELEMENTS
• • • • • • 24:00 JUNE 13
— • — • — 24:00 JUNE 14
— — — — 24:00 JUNE 15
▲▲▲▲▲▲ 24:00 JUNE 16
→ AXIS OF ADVANCE JUNE 14
BOUNDARIES AS OF JUNE 14

0 — 2 miles
0 — 2 km

Colomby

Urville

Le Ham
359th Inf

Montebourg Station

90th Div's new objective

Terre-de-Beauval

Golieville

Merderet R.

Grainville

Fresville

Le Port Bréhay

90
XX
9

1/47

Biniville

Hautteville-Bocage

Le Calais

358th Inf

358th Inf

Neuville-au-Plain

68th

Nèhou

Ste.-Colombe

3/47

2/47

Orglandes

39th

Gourbesville

359th Inf

357

June 16

La Fière bridge

Beauvais

Bigeville

47th Inf

Les Landes
359th Inf

Amfreville

Ste.-Mère-Eglise

La Fière

Reignaville

359th Inf

359th Inf

Le Motey

Cauquigny

Fouville

9
XX
82

60th Inf

60th Inf

359th Inf

507th PIR

Bohneville

Haut-Guetteville

50th

Chel-du-Pont

505th PIR

Reuville

Renouf

Château Haut

St.-Sauveur-le-Vicomté

325th

Gottol

Picauville

358th Inf

507th PIR

Eturville

Pont l'Abbé

325th GIR

Carquebut

508th PIR

Douve R.

Château L'Isle Marie

Étienville

Beuzeville-la-Bastille

Le Port

59

Left:
Memorial to the 300 US soldiers of the 82nd AB and 90th Infantry Div who died liberating Gourbesville, a village two miles west of La Fière. In the town's churchyard there is also a plaque dedicated to James R. Hattrick of the 508th PIR, who landed in Gourbesville, fought till he was killed, and was originally buried there.

Below left
A memorial in Picauville to the 9th Air Force and 82nd and 101st AB divisions. The site lists crashed aircraft (not counting gliders). To the left is a tribute to the 9th USAAF and RAF who were based at the airstrip in Picauville once the town had been liberated.

Above:
St. Sauveur-le-Vicomte taken.

Left:
Aid station at Etuienville.

Opposite, Below left:
A US company command conference on the bonnet of a Citroen in St. Saveur.

Opposite, Below right:
Capt. Briand Boaudin and Lt. Paul Lehman of the 82nd AB were captured on D-Day but liberated a few days later along with some German souvenirs (and confiscated French wine). Boaudin holds a leather-bound German medical valise which is now on display in the Airborne Museum at Fort Bragg.

Aftermath

Yet even with the Cotentin severed, the paratroopers were still not relieved. While Omar Bradley now directed Joe Collins' V Corps north toward Cherbourg, Troy Middleton's new VIII Corps would attack southward across the Douve River. In early July, against the wishes of Gavin and two regimental commanders, Gen. Ridgway agreed to have the 82nd AB spearhead the VIII Corps attack south toward La Haye-du-Puits. It was a matter of paratroop and glider companies down to less than half-strength leading the way for new, unblooded divisions..

Nevertheless, again the 82nd outstripped its flanking units until La Haye-du-Puits had fallen, a point at which the front solidified pending the main-force US offensive at Saint-Lô. On July 8, over a month after D-Day, the 82nd Airborne was finally relieved from the frontline and pulled back to England to prepare for its next mission, less nearly half its original numbers. Ridgway was subsequently promoted to command of the newly formed XVIII Airborne Corps while Jim Gavin took over the 82nd AB. The following weeks would be spent incorporating thousands of new volunteers churned out by US jump schools to join the now-famous 82nd Airborne paratroop elite. Scarcely two months would pass before they would jump behind enemy lines again, this time in Holland, in the operation codenamed Market Garden.

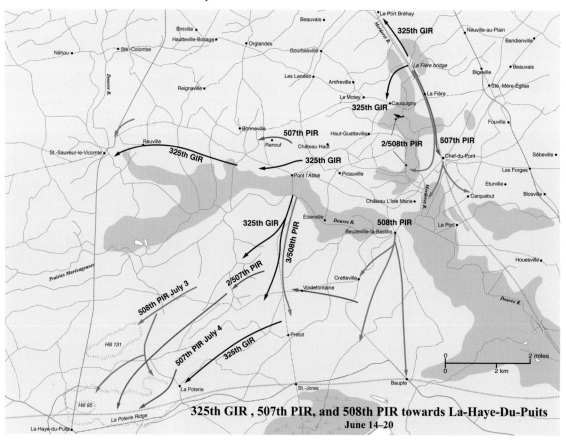

325th GIR , 507th PIR, and 508th PIR towards La-Haye-Du-Puits
June 14–20

The war memorial of Graignes commemorates the fallen civilians and soldiers who died after the invasion. At about 02:00 on June 6, 170 paratroopers of the 82nd landed near Graignes, some 12 miles south of their target, Amfreville. They took up positions in Graignes, the school becoming a command station and the church bell tower an observation post. There was little fighting until "Bloody Sunday"—June 11—when the Germans seized control, executing prisoners and civilians. Graignes was liberated the next day, although every building in the community was damaged.

Bibliography

Traces of War (http://en.tracesofwar.com) is a fount of knowledge about—memorials, fortifications, cemeteries, points of interest, awards: definitely worth checking out.

Alexander, M.J. and J. Sperry: *Jump Commander*; Casemate, 2012.

Booth, T.M. and D. Spencer: *Paratrooper*; Simon & Schuster, 1994.

Harrison, Gordon A.: *United States Army in World War II European Theater of Operations, Cross-Channel Attack*; retrieved from http://www.ibiblio.org/hyperwar/USA/USA-E-XChannel/index.html.

Lebenson, Len: *Surrounded by Heroes*; Casemate, 2007.

Marshall, S.L.A.: *Night Drop*; Atlantic Monthly, 1962.

Murphy, Robert M.: *No Better Place to Die*; Casemate, 2009.

Nordyke, Phil: *All American All the Way*; Zenith Press, 2005.

Whitlock, Flint: *If Chaos Reigns*; Casemate, 2011.

Verier, Mike: Spearhead 4: *82nd Airborne Division 'All American'*; Ian Allan Ltd, 2001.

Wurst, S.F. and G. Wurst: *Descending from the Clouds*; Casemate, 2004.

Above:

A booklet written and published by 82nd AB headquarters after its return to England, detailing the first few harrowing days of the invasion.

Below:

This memorial at the south end of Sainte-Mère-Église commemorates the landing of the paratroopers of the 505th PIR.

Key to Map Symbols